Old-Fashioned
HOMEMADE ICE CREAM

With 58 Original Recipes

THOMAS R. QUINN

DOVER PUBLICATIONS, INC.
NEW YORK

Old-Fashioned Homemade Ice Cream is a new work, first published by
Dover Publications, Inc., in 1984.

Manufactured in the United States of America
Dover Publications, Inc., 31 East 2nd Street, Mineola, N.Y. 11501

Library of Congress Cataloging in Publication Data

Quinn, Thomas R.
  Old-fashioned homemade ice cream.

  1. Ice cream, ices, etc.   I. Title.
TX795.Q57   1984   641.8'62   82-18260
ISBN 0-486-24495-4

CONTENTS

Introduction

Not so very long ago, ice cream was not something that came from the supermarket in a cardboard box, but a magical substance that you had to work to make from country cream, sugar, fresh eggs and flavorings. During regular family visits to my grandparents when I was a child, ice cream making was a favorite activity, and one that produced more results than most. Someone would bring out the old hand-cranked ice cream freezer, and then Grandma would make an ice cream mixture, usually a caramel or fruit flavor. Grandpa would put large chunks of ice into a gunny sack and break them up with a heavy mallet. Then all of the uncles, cousins and aunts would go down to the basement and help churn the ice cream, taking turns pouring in crushed ice, adding rock salt and turning the crank. As the mixture began to freeze, two of us would help hold down the ice cream bucket and make it easier to churn. When the mixture got so stiff that only Grandpa could still turn the crank, it was a signal to the kids that the dasher was about to be removed and we would get a taste of the ice cream.

It has been many years since I turned ice cream in the basement of my grandparents' house. During many of those years, the amount of ice cream produced at home in America diminished steadily. But in these days when people are returning to nature and producing more of their own food, home ice cream making is enjoying a revival. Old ice cream freezers are being dusted off and returned to use, and new ones are being manufactured and sold by the tens of thousands. But many family recipes for good home-churned ice cream have been lost. Grandmother may have made it by adding a little of this and a little of that, but the newcomer to homemade ice cream needs a recipe to follow, and even the experienced home ice cream maker can always use suggestions for new flavors and new combinations of ingredients. All the ice cream recipes in this book are intended to be churn-frozen in a home ice cream freezer. The quantities given will make about one gallon, unless otherwise noted. Home ice cream freezers come in all sizes, but fortunately no adjustments are necessary when reducing or expanding the recipes: you need only keep the proportion of ingredients the same when making any amount of ice cream. Don't hesitate to experiment, to try new recipes and to develop your own. Developing new and different taste sensations is part of the fun.

Ice Cream in the Old Days

Ice cream as we know it today is a relatively recent invention. The first beginnings of this kind of foodstuff are lost in history, but the Roman emperor Nero probably feasted on an ancestor of ice cream—snow mixed with honey and fruits—around 62 A.D. History tells us that water ices (frozen punches) were made in Italy in the fifteenth century. From water ices, recipes that contained milk or cream were eventually developed. In the seventeenth century, a French ice cream maker in the employ of King Charles I of England was paid to keep his recipe a royal secret. In 1769 *The Experienced English Housekeeper* printed the first known recipe for "cream ice." French and English cookbooks published in the early 1770's contained recipes for "cream ices" and "butter ices."

The first record of ice cream in America dates from 1700 when Governor Bladen of Maryland served it to some of his guests attending a dinner party. Philip Lenzi, a confectioner from London, made ice cream and advertised it for sale in New York City beginning in 1774. Ice cream remained an expensive delicacy, available only in confectioneries and cafés, for many years. Recipes were still a carefully guarded secret.

In 1848 the first U.S. patent was granted for a revolving hand-crank freezer with a dasher, one of the first to be made commercially in the United States.

It was not until 1851 that ice cream became available on the wholesale market. Jacob Fussell of Baltimore added ice cream to his line of wholesale dairy products, built the first ice cream manufacturing plant in Baltimore, and later expanded his business to Washington, D.C., New York and Boston.

Ice cream did not become really well known until the twentieth century, when mechanical refrigeration and changing economic conditions made it available to a wider market. The industry has made great strides in the last eighty-odd years. In 1904 the ice cream cone was introduced at the St. Louis World Fair. It wasn't until as recently as the 1940's that carry-home ice cream from grocery and candy stores gained in popularity, and soft ice cream appeared in drive-in sales outlets.

Today the amount of ice cream made at home is minuscule compared with the amount commercially produced. This book is dedicated to that fraction produced at home. May it melt slowly.

Ingredients: What They Do

The old saying, "You get out only what you put in," holds true for ice cream. The better the ingredients, the better the ice cream. Making good homemade ice cream is not inexpensive, but using inferior ingredients only leads to disappointment and wasted effort.

Milk and Milk Products

Milk and its products are the basic ingredients of ice cream. All recipes in this book utilize milk in various forms and quantities.

Milk, as it comes from the cow, with all the natural milk fats left in, is called whole milk. Whole milk purchased at the grocery store contains not less than 3.25% milk fat.

Milk fat or butterfat, as it is sometimes called, is the most important component of ice cream. Ice cream gets its rich, creamy flavor from milk fats. Fat also contributes to producing a smooth texture and a greater resistance to melting.

A milk-fat content between 14% and 22% is ideal for producing a rich-tasting, full-bodied ice cream. Ice cream made with less than 14% milk fat is weak-bodied, coarse and icy. With a milk-fat content much greater than 22% the ice cream is too buttery tasting and doesn't expand during the freezing process, thus reducing the yield.

Two percent milk, as its name implies, contains 2% milk fats. If two percent milk is used to make ice cream, more cream must be added to raise the total milk-fat content to desirable levels.

Skim milk contains no milk fats, making it necessary to use large quantities of cream to provide the amount of milk fat needed for good ice cream.

Half-and-half is half whole milk and half cream. Although the milk-fat content of half-and-half varies, it is around 12% to 20%, making it ideal for use in ice cream. Half-and-half is usually less expensive than whole milk and heavy cream bought separately. Half-and-half may be used in place of equal parts of heavy cream and whole milk in any recipe in this book.

Heavy cream, or whipping cream as it is usually called, contains 30–40% milk fats. Ice cream made using heavy cream as its milk source has a buttery taste. It is best to mix cream and some other form of milk to reduce the fat content.

Coffee cream, sometimes called light cream, varies in milk-fat content from 18% to 30%. Using a mixture of one-third whole milk and two-thirds coffee cream makes a rich-tasting, full-bodied ice cream.

Evaporated milk is whole milk with approximately 60% of the water taken out. Usually vitamin D is added. Evaporated milk has the same food value as whole milk, but more than twice the milk-fat content (8%). Because of its processing, it has a noticeable cooked flavor and caramelized color that is undesirable in most ice creams.

Sweetened condensed milk is made by removing about half of the water from whole milk and adding sugar. This product contains 40–45% sugar and has a milk-fat content of not less than 8.5%.

Many ice cream recipes found in older cookbooks require heating the milk to near boiling. This was done to pasteurize the milk, thus killing bacteria and improving the keeping quality of milk products. All milk purchased in stores nowadays has already been pasteurized, so it is no longer necessary to heat milk to such high temperatures and risk burning or scorching. The ice cream mixture does need to be heated to moderate temperatures, 110–160°, to cook the eggs, blend flavors and produce a more uniform product. A thermometer is useful for bringing the mixture to the right temperature.

Sugar and Sweeteners

How sweet it is depends on how much sugar or other sweetener is used. Good ice cream should contain 14–16% sugar. Depending on personal tastes, the sugar content can range from 12% to 29%.

The sugar content affects the smoothness and creamy flavor of ice cream. Too much sugar, and it becomes soggy and sticky, and more salt and ice are required to freeze it. Too little sugar, and ice cream tastes flat and can freeze very hard with little increase in volume. Flavor is also affected by the sugar content. A high sugar content overpowers the flavors of some fruits and other delicate flavors.

Eggs

Eggs give ice cream a rich-looking appearance and improve its flavor. The addition of eggs turns an average ice cream into a high-quality frozen dessert. Egg yolks improve the whipping ability of the ice cream mixture and produce a firmer-bodied product. They also contribute to a smooth texture and add a delicate flavor to ice cream. When cooked, eggs thicken the ice cream mixture and blend flavors.

NOTE: If eggs are not part of a given recipe, the mixture should be aged at least 24 hours in the refrigerator before freezing.

Rennet

Rennet is a thickening agent made from the enzyme rennin, found in the stomach lining of young cattle. Usually manufactured in tablet form, rennet is dissolved in water and added to the ice cream mixture 10 minutes before freezing. The mixture should be stirred only slightly after the rennet is added, because continued agitation will not allow the mixture to coagulate properly.

Ice cream with rennet added will be slightly firmer and have a smoother texture. Rennet is especially helpful if the milk-fat content of the ice cream is low, or if eggs are not used in the recipe. Rennet tablets can be found in the gelatin sections of most food stores.

Flavorings

The quality of the flavorings used in ice cream is very important. Only top-quality flavoring extracts can produce high-quality ice cream. Low-quality extracts can produce poor-tasting, off-flavored ice cream. Never attempt to cut costs by using inferior flavorings.

The most popular flavoring substances used in ice cream are vanilla, chocolate and cocoa, fruits, nuts and sugars. Coffee, liqueurs, spices and artificial flavorings are also used.

While tastes vary, most people prefer ice cream with a mild, delicate flavor, which is best produced with natural flavorings. Because of the composition of most natural flavorings, no unpleasant tastes develop even at high concentrations. Imitation flavorings, unless carefully used in small quantities, often impart an overpowering, objectionable taste.

Vanilla is the most popular flavor for ice cream. Well over half of all ice creams contain vanilla flavoring. It comes from the pods of several species of orchids of the genus *Vanilla*. The Aztecs are said to have used vanilla beans to add to the flavor of chocolate. Vanilla beans are picked and then fermented to develop the flavor.

Vanilla for flavoring is available as a bean pod, vanilla extract, vanilla powder or imitation flavoring.

Although relatively expensive, real vanilla beans make excellent vanilla ice cream. Split the bean pod lengthwise and cook with the milk and cream until just below the boiling point. Let the mixture cool and the vanilla flavor diffuse for at least 30 minutes. Strain the mixture to remove the bean residue. One inch of vanilla bean gives approximately the same flavor strength as one teaspoon of vanilla extract.

Vanilla beans can also be dried and ground into a very fine powder. Ice cream made with vanilla powder will contain small black specks of ground beans. Use one teaspoon of vanilla powder to substitute for one to two teaspoons of vanilla extract.

Vanilla extract is made by dissolving finely cut vanilla beans in an alcohol solution. Imitation vanilla flavoring contains no vanilla beans at all, but is made from synthetic vanillin. Imitation vanilla flavoring has a slightly different flavor from that which occurs naturally in vanilla beans. Vanilla extract and imitation vanilla flavoring are of equivalent strength. Measure imitation vanilla flavoring carefully, because if too much is used, an unpleasant taste will develop.

Chocolate (or cocoa), the second most popular flavoring for ice cream, comes from the tree *Theobroma cacao*. There are 20 to 60 beans to the fruit pod. When the pods turn a golden red in color they are ripe and are cut from the tree. The beans are removed from the pods and heated and fermented until the familiar cinnamon-red color develops. The beans are then washed, dried, roasted and crushed.

In order to incorporate the full flavor of chocolate into the ice cream mixture, the cocoa (or chocolate) should be combined with sugar and added to the milk or cream before heating. The heat incorporates the cocoa more evenly and produces a fuller-bodied flavor.

Fruit is a very popular ice cream flavoring, especially when in season. Fresh fruits should be diced or coarsely puréed before using. Large pieces of fruit will get caught in the dasher blades and not be distributed evenly. Sweeten fresh fruits with sugar and refrigerate at least 12 hours to give the flavors time to blend.

Nuts are used in many ice creams for added flavor. Almost any kind of nut can be used successfully. Nuts must be carefully chopped before they are added to the mixture; large pieces can damage the dasher and sides of the freezing can. Make sure the nuts used are free of hulls and not rancid.

Substituting Ingredients

The recipes in this book were carefully researched and tested to develop the best-tasting ice cream possible. To retain this tested flavor, use the exact ingredients called for if at all possible. Substituting ingredients is not recommended because unpredictable changes may occur in the ice cream. If, in an emergency, a substitution must be made, the following stand-in ingredients will usually produce an acceptable ice cream.

If You're Out of . . .	Use
1 square unsweetened baking chocolate	3 tablespoons cocoa plus 1 tablespoon butter or margarine
1 cup whole milk	½ cup evaporated milk plus ½ cup water, *or*
	1 cup reconstituted nonfat dry milk plus 1 tablespoon butter or margarine
1 whole egg	2 egg yolks
1 cup sugar	¾ cup honey (plus about one tablespoon gelatin per quart of liquid as thickener)
1 tablespoon cornstarch	2 tablespoons flour
1″ vanilla bean	1 teaspoon vanilla extract

The Freezing Process

The ice cream mixture freezes through the action of the rock salt and ice packed around it. When ice and salt are mixed, the moist surface of the ice dissolves the salt. This in turn lowers the melting point of the ice. The whole process rapidly reduces the temperature of the ice and water, and the ice cream mixture. The ice cream freezes.

Ice

It takes approximately 16 pounds of ice to freeze and pack one gallon of ice cream. Crushed or chipped ice is best. The coarser the ice, the longer the freezing time and the more rock salt needed.

Ice cubes do not present enough surface area to the freezing can, and the air spaces between them slow down the freezing process. Besides, most electric freezers will stall frequently if ice cubes are used; they get caught between the sides of the bucket and the freezing can, causing the motor to stop. If cube ice is all that is available, you can crush it by placing it in a heavy cloth bag and pounding it with the side of a hammer.

If you have a food freezer, or even the freezing compartment of a refrigerator, you can make your own ice. Miniature ice-cube trays make ice of a good size for freezing ice cream (regular-sized cubes must be broken into smaller pieces). Sixteen to twenty trays of ice will freeze one gallon of ice cream. Milk cartons can be washed, filled with water and frozen. When the ice is frozen, use an ice pick to break up the blocks, then crush them with a hammer.

Salt

Rock salt is preferable to table salt for freezing homemade ice cream. Table salt tends to form icy crusts that keep the ice from moving down in the freezer bucket. Rock salt is also less expensive than table salt.

2½–3 cups of rock salt will freeze a gallon of ice cream. Additional rock salt is needed to pack the ice cream after freezing. If you find yourself out of rock salt, table salt can be used. You will need to push the ice down in the bucket frequently to break up any ice bridges that may have formed.

Decrease the amount of salt if you are using table salt. The finer-grained table salt dissolves faster than rock salt and lowers the temperature of the ice cream mixture faster. Lowering the temperature too fast causes a coarse-textured, icy ice cream.

Freezers

The best ice cream freezer, whether a hand-crank or electric model, has a sturdy, well-insulated bucket. Poorly insulated buckets require more ice, salt and time to freeze ice cream. A well-insulated bucket helps to produce a firm, high-quality ice cream. Wooden buckets have good insulating qualities and are noncorrosive. Fiberglass buckets are durable and won't rust, but give up some insulating qualities. Plastic and metal buckets are poor insulators and may be subject to damage. Many buckets sold today have an outer wooden shell with a fiberglass or plastic liner. This combination of materials seems to produce a good, serviceable bucket.

The inner bucket, or freezing can, should be constructed of galvanized or stainless steel to prevent rusting. The freezing can takes a lot of punishment, both inside and out. It must be made of heavy-gauge material to withstand gouging from ice and denting by fruits and nuts that can get wedged between the dasher and the sides of the can.

The dasher churns the ice cream, either with an electric motor or by hand-cranking. Electric freezers take most of the work out of making homemade ice cream. Simply plug in the electric freezer, add ice and salt, and wait 20 to 30 minutes until the motor sounds heavily burdened.

Hand-cranking ice cream, besides building muscles, often becomes a social event. The whole family or social gathering takes turns in the labor in order to enjoy the final product. Ice cream seems to taste just a bit better if you have to work a little to freeze it.

Hand-cranked freezers also have the advantage of being able to produce a smoother ice cream than electric freezers. By varying the speed of the dasher, first turning slowly and then faster as the ice cream mixture begins to freeze, a smoother texture is produced.

For those who enjoy camping and picnicking where electricity may not be available, a hand-cranked freezer can be a welcome piece of equipment.

Freezing Ice Cream in a Home Ice Cream Freezer

1. Make sure all parts of the freezer (dasher, freezing can and cover) are thoroughly clean. Bacteria thrive on the ingredients of ice cream.

2. Ice cream should be turned where the salt water draining from the bucket will not cause damage. A laundry tub or sink is ideal. When turning ice cream outdoors, the salt water should be drained away from cement, grass and flowers.

3. Adjust the dasher so it fits snugly against the sides of the freezing can. Put the dasher in the freezing can and fill with cool ice cream mixture to within no more than 3 or 4 inches from the top. Ice cream expands during the freezing process.

4. Put the lid on the freezing can. Make sure it is tight so salt will not leak into the can.

5. Place the freezing can inside the ice bucket and secure the hand crank or electric motor.

6. Pour about one quart of cold water into the bottom of the ice bucket. (For half-gallon freezers, use two cups of cold water.)

7. Fill the ice bucket one-third full with crushed or chipped ice.

8. Pour about ¾ cup of rock salt on top of the ice.

9. Continue adding layers of ice and salt until the ice is level with the top of the freezing can. Add about 3″ of ice and ⅓ cup of salt for each layer.

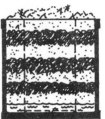

Salt and ice should be added in alternate layers.

10. *For Hand-Crank Freezer:* Begin turning the crank so that the freezing can rotates about one revolution per second. When the crank starts to get hard to turn, speed up the revolutions to about two per second. This beats air into the ice cream, making it smooth and creamy. You will not be able to keep this speed up until the ice cream is completely hardened. It will get too difficult to turn.
For Electric Freezer: Plug the electric motor in to a grounded outlet.

11. Keep the bucket full by continually adding ice and salt. About 16 pounds of ice and 2½ cups of rock salt will be used to freeze one gallon of ice cream.

12. Check the drain hole occasionally to make sure it isn't blocked. During the latter stages of the freezing process, salt water (brine) will flow from the drain hole.

13. *For Hand-Crank Freezer:* Continue turning the crank until it is very difficult to turn. One person will need to hold down the bucket while another turns the crank. The freezing process will take about 25 minutes.
For Electric Freezer: When the electric motor stalls or slows to almost a stop (follow manufacturer's directions), unplug it. The freezing process will take about 25 minutes.

14. Pour off some of the water and remove the ice from around the top of the freezing can.

15. Remove the crank or electric motor. Wipe off and remove the freezing-can lid.

16. Slowly pull the dasher out of the freezing can. Use a rubber spatula to scrape the ice cream off the dasher. (This is a good time to taste what you have made!)

17. After removing the dasher, use the spatula to push the ice cream down in the freezer to remove air pockets.

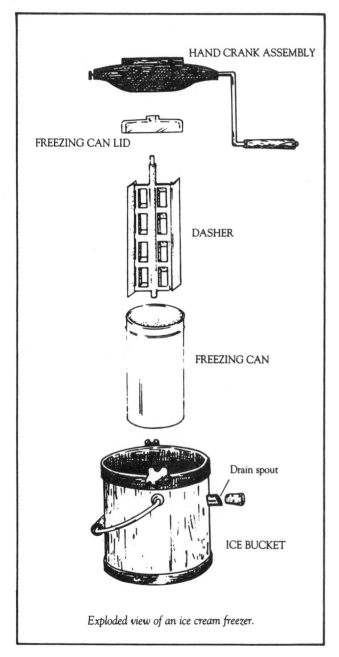

HAND CRANK ASSEMBLY

FREEZING CAN LID

DASHER

FREEZING CAN

Drain spout

ICE BUCKET

Exploded view of an ice cream freezer.

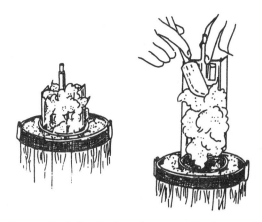

Remove the dasher slowly and scrape it off with a spatula.

18. Replace the lid and plug the hole with a cork.
19. Repack the ice bucket with layers of ice and rock salt.
20. Cover the ice bucket with an old rug, a blanket or anything that will help hold the cold in.
21. Let the ice cream set and harden for 3 or 4 hours or as long as you can wait.

Serving Temperature

The serving temperature of ice cream affects the flavor intensity and sweetness. Most people prefer ice cream served at 8°F. The flavor becomes more intense and sweeter at warmer serving temperatures. Sweet ice creams and ice creams with strong flavors taste best when served at colder temperatures.

Storing Homemade Ice Cream

After making ice cream, you can pack it in airtight containers for later enjoyment. Most flavors of homemade ice cream will become quite hard when refrozen. Letting the ice cream sit at room temperature for a few minutes will soften it enough for easy dipping. Homemade ice cream can be stored in the freezing compartment of your refrigerator for up to two weeks. If it is kept longer, ice crystals begin to form, and the quality deteriorates rapidly.

My Ice Cream Flopped! What Went Wrong?

Coarse and icy
1. Not enough cream was used (too low a milk-fat content).
2. Too much table salt was used, causing the ice cream mixture to freeze too rapidly. (Homemade ice cream should take 20 to 30 minutes to freeze.)
3. The dasher did not turn fast enough during the freezing stage, and not enough air was beaten into the mixture.
4. The ice cream mixture was frozen without agitation.
5. The ice cream thawed and was refrozen.
6. A recipe without eggs was used and the mixture was not aged at least 24 hours in the refrigerator before freezing.

Did not freeze
1. Not enough rock salt was used. (About 2½ cups of rock salt is needed to freeze one gallon of ice cream.)
2. Too much sugar was used.

3. Uncooked pineapple was used.
4. Honey was substituted for sugar (unflavored gelatin must be added as a thickener if honey is used).

Weak and mushy body
1. Not enough cream was used (too low a milk-fat content).
2. Too much sugar was used.
3. The dasher wasn't turning fast enough during the freezing stage to beat air into the mixture.
4. Eggs were omitted from the recipe.
5. Too low a milk-solid content.

Off-flavor
1. Rancid nuts were used.
2. Cream or milk was spoiled.
3. Inferior flavoring was used.

Vanilla Ice Cream Recipes

Five-Star Vanilla Ice Cream

This recipe is the result of many experiments. As my friends can attest, not all of the first experimental recipes were edible. Many of the recipes in this book are variations of Five-Star Vanilla Ice Cream.

  2⅔ cups granulated sugar
  4 eggs
  7 cups whole milk
  3 cups whipping cream
  8 teaspoons vanilla extract
  5 rennet tablets dissolved in ¼ cup cold water

In a large kettle or Dutch oven, combine the sugar and eggs to make a paste. Add the milk and cream. Heat over medium-low heat, stirring constantly to prevent scorching the milk. Remove from the heat when the mixture reaches 110°F.

   The mixture should cool in the refrigerator for at least an hour. This reduces the freezing time and will save a considerable amount of ice. Add the vanilla to the mixture when it has cooled.

   Pour the cooled mixture into the freezing can. Stir the dissolved rennet tablets into the mixture. Leave undisturbed ten minutes. Churn and freeze in an ice cream freezer. Makes about one gallon.

Mother's Vanilla Ice Cream

Remember how good Mother's homemade ice cream tasted? Everyone would gather on the back porch on a Sunday afternoon to turn the crank on the ice cream freezer and lick the dasher when it was removed. If your mother didn't make homemade ice cream, this recipe will help make up for it. Give it a try, especially if you like a sweeter ice cream.

  4 eggs, lightly beaten
  2⅔ cups sugar
  6 cups whole milk
  2 cans evaporated milk
  ⅔ cup sweetened condensed milk
  4 teaspoons vanilla
  6 rennet tablets dissolved in ¼ cup cold water

Combine the eggs, sugar and 3 cups of the whole milk in a large pan. Cook and stir the mixture over medium-low heat until lukewarm (110°F).

   Remove from heat and add the evaporated milk, the sweetened condensed milk, the vanilla and the remainder of the whole milk. Refrigerate the mixture until it has cooled to at least room temperature.

   Dissolve the rennet tablets in cold water. Stir the dissolved tablets into the ice cream mixture and let stand undisturbed for 10 minutes. Immediately freeze the ice cream. Makes about one gallon.

French Vanilla Ice Cream

French Vanilla Ice Cream is distinguished by lots of eggs and plenty of cream. It is a rich, custardlike ice cream of the finest quality. This particular recipe also uses vanilla beans instead of vanilla extract. French Vanilla is the ice cream of gourmets.

    2 vanilla beans or 2 tablespoons vanilla extract
    2 quarts half-and-half
    2⅓ cups sugar
    12 egg yolks
    2 cups whipping cream
    ¼ teaspoon salt

Cut the vanilla beans in half lengthwise. Add, seeds and all, to the half-and-half. Stirring constantly, slowly heat the mixture until it is almost boiling (about 200°F). Remove the pan from the heat and let stand at least 30 minutes to allow the vanilla flavor to blend in with the milk. Then remove the bean pods and strain the mixture.

In a small mixing bowl, combine the sugar and egg yolks to make a paste. Return the milk mixture to low heat and stir in the sugar, egg yolks, whipping cream and salt. Cook and stir until the mixture is thick enough to coat the back of a wooden spoon. Remove from the heat and chill in the refrigerator. If you are not using vanilla beans, now is the time to add the vanilla extract.

Freeze in an ice cream freezer. Makes about one gallon.

Corn Syrup Vanilla Ice Cream

If your kitchen cupboard is running low on granulated sugar, or if you just want to try something different, this recipe uses light corn syrup as a partial replacement for sugar. Corn Syrup Vanilla Ice Cream has a slightly different taste and finer-grained texture because of the partial substitution of corn syrup for granulated sugar. It also will not freeze as firmly as ordinary sugar-based ice cream.

    1⅓ cups granulated sugar
    4 eggs
    5 cups whole milk
    ⅛ teaspoon salt
    2½ cups light corn syrup
    3 cups whipping cream
    8 teaspoons vanilla

In a large pan combine the sugar and eggs to make a paste. Slowly add the milk and heat to approximately 180°F, stirring constantly to prevent scorching. Remove from heat and immediately stir in the salt, corn syrup and then the cream and vanilla.

Refrigerate the mixture until it is cool.

Freeze in an ice cream freezer. Makes about one gallon.

Easy No-Cook Vanilla Ice Cream

More homemade vanilla ice cream is made than any other flavor. The following recipe for Easy Vanilla Ice Cream is made without eggs or cooking. Sweetened condensed milk adds a special creaminess and body to this ice cream. Because no cooking is needed, this recipe is good to make while on picnics or while camping.

    1 quart whipping cream
    6 cups whole milk
    1 14-ounce can sweetened condensed milk
    1 cup sugar
    2 tablespoons vanilla
    ⅛ teaspoon salt

Pour all of the ingredients into an ice cream freezing can and freeze. Makes about one gallon.

Chocolate Ice Cream Recipes

Creamy Chocolate Ice Cream

There is hardly a child or an adult around who doesn't like chocolate. After vanilla, chocolate ice cream is by far the most popular flavor. Even vanilla ice cream is often transformed by chocolate syrup or hot fudge.

    1½ cups cocoa
    2⅔ cups granulated sugar
    4 eggs
    about 5 cups whole milk
    3 cups whipping cream
    5 rennet tablets dissolved in ¼ cup cold water
    4 teaspoons vanilla

Blend together the cocoa and sugar, and stir in the eggs to make a paste. Slowly add 1 quart whole milk and 3 cups whipping cream. Heat the mixture over medium-low heat, stirring to prevent scorching. Remove from heat when mixture reaches about 160°F, and refrigerate until cool. Add vanilla and enough whole milk to fill the freezing can ¾ full.

Add the dissolved rennet tablets ten minutes before churning in an ice cream freezer. Makes about one gallon.

Sweet German Chocolate Ice Cream

On a scale of one to ten, Sweet German Chocolate Ice Cream is a ten plus. It has a sweet, velvety taste that no other chocolate ice cream can match, with small flakes of chocolate suspended in a delicious chocolate cream.

    4 eggs
    2⅔ cups sugar
    8 1-ounce squares Baker's German Sweet chocolate
    1 quart half-and-half
    1 quart whole milk
    4 teaspoons vanilla

Blend the eggs and sugar together to make a paste. Over a medium-low flame, heat the eggs, sugar, chocolate squares and half-and-half. Heat and stir until the chocolate squares have melted and the mixture reaches approximately 160°F. Remove from the heat and refrigerate until cool. Add the vanilla and whole milk. Freeze in an ice cream freezer. Makes about one gallon.

Choo Choo Chocolate Ice Cream

This is the king of the chocolate ice creams. Choo Choo Chocolate Ice Cream is rich, creamy and oh, so chocolaty. Made with unsweetened chocolate, this recipe will put a smile on any chocolate-lover's face.

    6 1-ounce squares unsweetened chocolate
    ½ cup cold water
    2½ cups sugar
    4 eggs, lightly beaten
    4 cups whole milk
    ⅛ teaspoon salt
    4 cups whipping cream
    2 tablespoons vanilla extract

High temperatures destroy the flavor of chocolate. To preserve its delicate taste, either melt the unsweetened chocolate squares in the top of a double boiler, or break the chocolate into small pieces and add ½ cup cold water. Stir over low heat until the chocolate melts and forms a thick paste. Be careful not to burn the chocolate.

When the chocolate squares have melted, stir in the sugar, eggs, milk and salt. Continue to cook over low heat until the mixture blends and forms a smooth liquid. Stir constantly to avoid scorching or burning. A slow, gentle heat will thoroughly melt the chocolate, while high temperatures could destroy the chocolate flavor.

When the chocolate mixture is well blended, remove it from the heat and refrigerate. When cool, add the whipping cream and vanilla extract.

Freeze in an ice cream freezer. Makes about one gallon.

Mexican Spiced Chocolate Ice Cream

An excellent-tasting ice cream, Mexican Spiced Chocolate is rich and creamy smooth. Flakes of chocolate dot this south-of-the-border-style ice cream. Mexican Spiced Chocolate Ice Cream keeps well when stored in an airtight container in your freezing compartment.

    3 ounces unsweetened baking chocolate
    1 quart whole milk
    2 teaspoons ground cinnamon
    ½ teaspoon ground ginger
    ½ teaspoon salt
    2½ cups sugar
    6 eggs
    1 quart whipping cream
    4 teaspoons vanilla extract
    ½ teaspoon almond extract

Melt the chocolate squares in a large pan over low heat, then stir in the milk, cinnamon, ginger and salt and in-

crease the heat to medium-low. Stir and heat until well blended.

In a mixing bowl blend together the sugar and eggs to make a thick paste. Pour the combined sugar and eggs into the milk mixture. Cook and stir until the mixture thickens (about 15 minutes and 170°F). Remove the mixture from the heat and refrigerate until cool (35°–40°F).

Add the whipping cream, vanilla and almond extract. Freeze in an ice-cream freezer. Makes about one gallon.

Jamoca Chocolate Ice Cream

Coffee is becoming an increasingly popular flavor for ice cream as well as for many other desserts. South American coffee plants and cocoa beans are often planted on the same plantation, if not side by side. Maybe this explains why Jamoca Chocolate Ice Cream tastes so naturally good.

    1 cup cocoa
    4 teaspoons instant coffee
    2⅔ cups sugar
    4 eggs
    about 6 cups whole milk
    3 cups whipping cream
    2 tablespoons vanilla extract

Blend together the cocoa, instant coffee, sugar and eggs. Slowly stir in 1 quart of whole milk and the whipping cream. Cook the mixture over medium-low heat for 12 to 15 minutes to blend the flavors and thicken. Stir often to prevent scorching. Remove from heat and refrigerate. When cool, add the vanilla. Pour the mixture into the freezing can. Add enough whole milk to fill the can ¾ full. Churn and freeze. Makes about one gallon.

Chocolate Banana Ice Cream

Have you ever had two things you really liked, but had to make a choice between the two? In my younger days my parents often took me out to a soft ice cream drive-in. I loved chocolate milk shakes, but I couldn't resist a milk shake made with slices of bananas, either. Aware of my predicament, the lady working at the drive-in suggested I order a milk shake flavored with both chocolate and bananas. It tasted great, and so does this Chocolate Banana Ice Cream recipe. If you, like me, cannot decide which flavor you like better, Chocolate Banana Ice Cream is for you.

    2⅔ cups sugar
    ⅔ cup cocoa
    4 eggs
    3 cups whipping cream
    about 5 cups whole milk
    2 cups mashed bananas (3 bananas)
    2 teaspoons vanilla

Mix the sugar, cocoa and eggs together in a large pan. While stirring, slowly add the whipping cream and half the milk. Cook and stir to about 110°F over medium-low heat. Remove from heat and refrigerate.

When cool, add the mashed bananas and vanilla. The bananas can be puréed in the blender or mashed with a potato masher. Pour the mixture into freezing can, adding whole milk to fill ¾ full. Freeze in an ice cream freezer. Makes about one gallon.

Chocolate Almond Ice Cream

To toast the almonds as called for in this recipe, spread chopped almonds in a single layer in a shallow baking pan. Put the pan under the broiler. When the almonds are just beginning to brown, turn them over in the pan and return them to the broiler so the other side can brown. Watch the almonds carefully: they will brown very fast.

   1⅓ cups cocoa
   2½ cups granulated sugar
   6 eggs
   1 quart whole milk
   1 quart whipping cream
   4 teaspoons vanilla
   ½ pound toasted almonds, finely chopped (1⅓ cups)

Blend together the cocoa and sugar. Add the eggs and stir until a smooth paste forms.

Add the milk to the mixture and cook over medium-low heat, stirring constantly. Heat until the mixture is very hot to the touch (about 150°F). Remove from the heat and refrigerate until cool.

When you are ready to freeze the ice cream, lightly beat together the whipping cream and vanilla. Fold into the chocolate mixture. Add the toasted almonds.

Freeze in an ice cream freezer. Makes about one gallon.

Nutty Chocolate Malt Ice Cream

Nutty Chocolate Malt Ice Cream tastes like a frozen chocolate malted milk with nuts. Kids love it!

   2⅔ cups sugar
   1 cup cocoa
   1 cup chocolate-flavored malted milk powder
   4 eggs
   3 pints half-and-half
   ½ cup finely chopped salted Spanish peanuts
   1 tablespoon vanilla
   whole milk as needed (about 2 cups)

Thoroughly combine the sugar, cocoa and chocolate malted milk powder in a large pan. Stir in the eggs to make a paste. Add the half-and-half. Cook over medium-low heat while stirring constantly. Remove from the heat when

the cocoa is well blended and the mixture is very hot, but not boiling (about 160°F). Remove from heat and refrigerate until cool.

When the mixture is cold and you are ready to freeze it, add the chopped peanuts, vanilla and enough milk to fill the freezing can ¾ full. Freeze in a home ice cream freezer. Makes about one gallon.

Bit o' Chocolate Ice Cream

Bit o' Chocolate Ice Cream by any other name would be chocolate chip, but this isn't ordinary black and white chocolate chip ice cream. Semisweet flakes of chocolate are suspended in a light, creamy chocolate ice cream.

   2⅔ cups sugar
   4 eggs
   6 cups whole milk
   3 cups whipping cream
   2 tablespoons vanilla
   2 cups (10 1-ounce squares) semisweet chocolate, shaved

In a large pan, blend together the sugar and eggs to make a paste. Add half the milk and all the cream. Bring the mixture to about 110°F over medium-low heat, stirring constantly to avoid scorching. Remove from the stove and refrigerate.

With a sharp knife, shave small pieces from the squares of semisweet chocolate.

Make sure the milk mixture is completely cooled before adding the shaved chocolate and vanilla. Pour the ice cream mixture into the freezing can, adding whole milk to fill to the proper level.

Freeze in an ice cream freezer. Makes about one gallon.

NOTE: Two cups of miniature semisweet chocolate chips may be used in place of the shaved semisweet squares. Regular-sized chocolate chips should not be used, as they could get caught on the dasher and damage the freezer.

Double Chocolate Chip Ice Cream

Doubly delicious, Double Chocolate Chip Ice Cream will drive chocolate lovers wild. It is a rich, velvety chocolate ice cream strewn with delectable chocolate morsels.

   1¼ cups cocoa
   2⅔ cups sugar
   4 eggs
   1 quart whole milk
   3 cups whipping cream
   2 tablespoons vanilla extract
   1½ cups semisweet chocolate, shaved (7½ squares)

Combine the cocoa, sugar and eggs in a large pan. Add the whole milk. Cook over medium-low heat, stirring to prevent scorching. Remove from heat after the mixture thickens (about 160°F). Cool in the refrigerator. With a sharp knife, shave the semisweet chocolate squares into very small pieces.

Before freezing, add the whipping cream, vanilla extract and shaved semisweet chocolate. The mixture must be cool or the shaved chocolate will melt.

Freeze in an ice cream freezer. Makes about one gallon.

NOTE: Miniature semisweet chocolate chips may be used in place of the shaved semisweet squares.

Mint Chocolate Chip Ice Cream

The flavor of mint perks up the taste buds and adds pizazz to chocolate chip ice cream. This ice cream is a refreshing climax to a heavy meal.

    2⅔ cups granulated sugar
    4 eggs
    7 cups whole milk
    2 cups whipping cream
    2 cups (10 1-ounce squares) semisweet chocolate,
        shaved
    2 teaspoons crème de menthe flavoring
    2 tablespoons vanilla

Combine the sugar and eggs to make a paste. Blend in the milk and whipping cream. Heat over medium-low heat, stirring frequently to avoid scorching. Remove from heat after the mixture has reached about 110°F (hot to touch). Refrigerate until the mixture has cooled. With a sharp knife, shave the semisweet chocolate squares into very small pieces.

When the milk mixture is cold, add the shaved chocolate, crème de menthe flavoring and vanilla. Freeze in an ice cream freezer. Makes about one gallon.

NOTE: Miniature semisweet chocolate chips may be used in place of the shaved semisweet squares.

Chocolate Swirl Ice Cream

Chocolate Swirl Ice Cream is a very appealing frozen dessert. Made from chocolate syrup and vanilla ice cream, it is easy to prepare. The chocolate swirl takes this ice cream out of the ordinary and puts it into the fancy dessert category.

All you need to make Chocolate Swirl Ice Cream is three cups of chocolate syrup and a gallon of vanilla ice cream. You can use either your favorite vanilla ice cream recipe or the recipe that follows.

    2½ cups sugar
    4 eggs
    7 cups half-and-half

    2 cups whole milk
    2 tablespoons vanilla extract
    3 cups chocolate syrup

Mix the sugar and eggs together well in a large pan. Add the half-and-half; heat over a medium-low flame, stirring constantly until the mixture is very hot (about 150°F). Remove from the heat and refrigerate until cool. Add the whole milk and vanilla before freezing. Freeze the mixture as you normally would. After freezing pack the ice cream for 2 to 3 hours to allow it to firm up (ripen).

When the ice cream has ripened, remove it from the freezing can. Repack it in layers in a container with an airtight lid. Alternate thin layers of ice cream and chocolate syrup. Serve immediately or store in the freezing section of your refrigerator. Makes about one gallon.

Fudge Royal Ice Cream

Drizzle it, swirl it, twirl it, strew it. Any way you do it, chocolate marbled ice cream is bowl-scraping good. Use your favorite vanilla ice cream recipe or the recipe below and freeze as usual. When the ice cream is frozen, remove it from the freezing can and repack it in thin layers in a freezer carton. Alternate layers of ice cream with thinned chocolate fudge poured in between. Use about 2½ cups of thinned chocolate fudge for each gallon of ice cream.

    9 cups half-and-half
    2⅓ cups sugar
    2 tablespoons vanilla extract
    ⅛ teaspoon salt
    2½ cups chocolate fudge topping

Pour all the ingredients except the chocolate fudge into the ice cream freezing can. Freeze as you would usually freeze ice cream. When it is frozen remove the dasher and repack the ice bucket with ice and salt. Allow the ice cream to harden 2 to 3 hours. Remove the ice cream from the freezing can and put into another container, alternating layers of ice cream and chocolate fudge. Makes about one gallon.

VARIATION: Add 1 cup of finely chopped Spanish peanuts to the mixture before freezing. When frozen, layer in the chocolate fudge and you will have created **Tin Roof Ice Cream.**

Chocolate Marshmallow Bits Ice Cream

Eating Chocolate Marshmallow Bits Ice Cream is like going on a treasure hunt looking for goodies. You eat your way through creamy chocolate ice cream looking for a marshmallow tidbit to sink your teeth into. This treasure hunt, however, is won by the person who savors the ice cream the longest.

1½ cups cocoa
2½ cups sugar
5 eggs
1 quart half-and-half
¼ teaspoon salt
4 teaspoons vanilla extract
2 cups miniature marshmallows, diced (cut up with
    scissors)
about 3 cups whole milk

Blend the cocoa and sugar in a large pan. Add the eggs and stir until a thick paste is made, then add the half-and-half and salt. Heat the mixture over medium-low heat, stirring constantly. When the mixture reaches about 140°F, remove it from the heat and refrigerate until cool.

Just before freezing the mixture in an ice cream freezer, add the vanilla, marshmallows and just enough whole milk to fill the freezing can to ¾ full. Makes about one gallon.

Chocolate Marshmallow Swirl Ice Cream

To make Chocolate Marshmallow Swirl Ice Cream you will need the recipe for your favorite homemade chocolate ice cream (or use the recipe below) and about 3 cups of marshmallow sauce. After freezing the chocolate ice cream, repack it in a freezer carton, alternating thin layers of ice cream with marshmallow sauce. Presto! Chocolate Marshmallow Swirl Ice Cream.

1½ cups cocoa
2 cups granulated sugar
⅛ teaspoon salt
3 eggs
½ cup sweetened condensed milk
6 cups half-and-half
2 cups whole milk
4 teaspoons vanilla extract

Thoroughly combine the cocoa, sugar and salt in a large pan. Stir in the eggs to make a thick paste. Add the sweetened condensed milk and half-and-half. Cook over medium-low heat until the mixture is well blended and very hot to touch (about 140°F). Remove the mixture from the heat, and refrigerate until cool. When you are ready to freeze the ice cream mixture, add the whole milk and vanilla. Makes about one gallon.

Making the Marshmallow Sauce
Method A: Combine about ½ cup of milk with a 7-ounce jar of marshmallow creme. Slowly heat in the top of a double boiler until the mixture is of pouring consistency. Pour in layers over ice cream while the marshmallow sauce is still warm.

Makes about 1½ cups. Double this recipe for one gallon of ice cream.

Method B: Over low heat, melt about 48 large marshmallows in 1 cup of milk. Stir until the marshmallows are completely melted, then remove the mixture from the heat. Use the marshmallow sauce while it is still warm and will pour.

Makes enough sauce for one gallon of ice cream.

Fruit Ice Cream Recipes

Apple Cinnamon Ice Cream

Ask them in the city. Ask them in the country. Everyone knows the number one pie in America is apple, and chances are, there is a scoop of ice cream on top of it. This recipe tastes like apple pie à la mode, hold the crust.

Apple Cinnamon Ice Cream can be made using chunky apple sauce, available in larger grocery stores, or made from scratch. A tart apple, such as Cortland or Mc-Intosh, makes good apple sauce. Peel, core and slice three apples. Cook them in ¾ cup cold water over medium heat until boiling. Reduce the heat, cover and simmer until the apples are soft (about 8 minutes). Add ⅓ cup brown sugar, ¼ teaspoon cinnamon and ⅛ teaspoon nutmeg. Bring to a boil while stirring constantly. Do not stir all of the lumps out; small pieces of apple should remain.

    2⅔ cups packed brown sugar
    ¼ cup cornstarch
    4 teaspoons cinnamon, or more to taste
    ⅛ teaspoon salt
    7 cups half-and-half
    2⅔ cups chunky apple sauce
    2 tablespoons lemon juice

Combine the dry ingredients (brown sugar, cornstarch, cinnamon and salt) in a large pan. Add the half-and-half; stir over medium-low heat until the mixture thickens. Remove from heat. Let the mixture cool slightly before adding the chunky apple sauce and lemon juice. Refrigerate to cool the mixture and blend the flavors. Freeze in an ice cream freezer. Makes about one gallon.

Chunky Apple Rum Ice Cream

A delightful flavor—small chunks of apple strewn in a light rum cream. Chunky Apple Rum Ice Cream is interestingly different from the usual fare, and wins a blue ribbon for taste and creativity. This recipe uses apple sauce with small pieces of apple. Smooth apple sauce will not work; you can either make your own chunky apple sauce or purchase it already prepared.

    2½ cups packed dark brown sugar
    ¼ cup cornstarch
    ⅛ teaspoon salt
    2 quarts half-and-half
    2⅔ cups chunky apple sauce
    2 tablespoons lemon juice
    1 teaspoon rum flavoring

In a large pan blend the brown sugar, cornstarch and salt. Add the half-and-half and cook over medium-low heat, stirring constantly. Cook until it thickens noticeably, then remove from heat and refrigerate until cool.

Just before freezing in an ice cream freezer, add the chunky apple sauce, lemon juice and rum flavoring. Makes about one gallon.

Banana Ice Cream

The banana is one of the most ancient cultivated plants known, and, with its close cousin the plantain, is a staple food in tropical countries around the world. Although it looks like a palm, the banana tree is really a huge herb, growing 10 to 20 feet high.

    5 cups whole milk
    4 eggs, lightly beaten
    2½ cups sugar
    dash of salt
    2 teaspoons vanilla
    2 cups mashed bananas (3 bananas)
    3 cups whipping cream

In a large pan, combine the milk, eggs, sugar and salt. While stirring, slowly heat the mixture until it coats the back of a wooden spoon. Do not boil. Remove from the heat and refrigerate until cool.

When ready to freeze the ice cream, stir in the vanilla, mashed bananas and whipping cream. Freeze in an ice cream freezer. Makes about one gallon.

Butterscotch Banana Ice Cream

My favorite pie, the one my mother always used to make for me on special occasions, is butterscotch banana, made from ripe bananas and butterscotch pudding. The butterscotch pudding must be made from scratch—from brown sugar, milk, egg yolks, cornstarch, salt, butter and vanilla. I still love butterscotch banana pie. But a close substitute, with the same great taste, is Butterscotch Banana Ice Cream. This ice cream uses the same ingredients as mother's butterscotch pudding. Now I can have my Butterscotch Banana Ice Cream on top of my butterscotch banana pie!

    2⅔ cups packed dark brown sugar
    ½ cup (1 stick) butter or margarine
    5½ cups whole milk
    3 cups whipping cream
    4 egg yolks, lightly beaten
    dash of salt
    5 teaspoons vanilla
    2 bananas, mashed (1⅔ cups)

Melt the butter over low heat in a large pan. Add the brown sugar and stir until the sugar just begins to caramelize. Turn the heat up to medium-low and add the milk, cream, egg yolks and salt. Cook the mixture until it is very hot (about 160°F). Continually stir the mixture while it is cooking to avoid scorching. When the cold milk and cream hit the mixture of warm butter and brown sugar, the butter may become lumpy and float to the top. As you continue to stir and the temperature of the mixture increases, the lumps will dissolve.

After the mixture has cooked, remove from heat and refrigerate until cool.

Mash the bananas either in a blender or with a potato masher.

Before freezing, add the vanilla and mashed bananas. Churn and freeze. Makes about one gallon.

Blackberry Ice Cream

Blackberries grow on a small shrub belonging to the rose family. Found wild in many parts of the United States, blackberries are a favorite food of wild animals, as well as man. Blackberry Ice Cream has a mild flavor compared to raspberry and other fruit-flavored ice creams. Nonetheless, Blackberry Ice Cream will have people licking their bowls clean and asking for more.

    2½ cups granulated sugar
    3 eggs
    6 cups half-and-half
    ¼ teaspoon salt
    2 teaspoons vanilla
    2 12-ounce packages of frozen blackberries (or about
        5 cups whole blackberries)
    sugar to sweeten blackberries lightly (about 1 cup)
    1 tablespoon lemon juice

Mix together the sugar and eggs to make a thick paste. Add the half-and-half and salt; heat in a large pan over a medium-low flame. Cook and stir until the mixture is very hot, but not boiling. Then remove from the stove and refrigerate. Stir in the vanilla when the mixture is cool.

Thaw two 12-ounce packages of blackberries, or use 5 cups of fresh or canned berries. Mash the blackberries with a potato masher. Sweeten to taste; about 1 cup of sugar should be adequate. You should have about 3 to 3½ cups of mashed, sweetened berries to mix into the ice cream. Stir the lemon juice into the berries and refrigerate overnight to allow time for the sugar to blend in well with the blackberries.

When ready to freeze, add the blackberries to the ice cream mixture. Freeze in an ice cream freezer. Makes about one gallon.

Blueberry Ice Cream

A favorite summer pastime in the Upper Peninsula of Michigan is picking wild blueberries, a common plant in the area that grows up to a foot tall. In July, people tramp the woods and open meadows looking for blueberries, although fighting off mosquitoes and blackflies can take as much time as picking the plump, bluish-black berries. Blueberries make a very pretty ice cream, and the taste lives up to its appearance.

    3 cups mashed blueberries, fresh, canned or frozen,
        sweetened with about ½ cup sugar (2 12-ounce
        packages frozen)
    2 tablespoons lemon juice
    2⅔ cups granulated sugar
    4 eggs
    7 cups half-and-half
    2 teaspoons vanilla

Mash the blueberries with a potato masher. Add the lemon juice and enough sugar (about ½ cup) to reduce the tartness. Refrigerate overnight.

In a large pan combine the sugar and eggs. Add the half-and-half and heat slowly for 12 to 15 minutes over medium-low heat until hot, but not boiling. Stir constantly to prevent scorching. Do not boil. Remove from the heat and refrigerate until the mixture is cold. Add the vanilla and blueberries. Freeze in an ice cream freezer. Makes about one gallon.

Orange Blossom Ice Cream

Orange Blossom Ice Cream is a thirst-quenching frozen dessert that helps to beat the summer heat, and also makes a great-tasting drink. By mixing ginger ale and Orange Blossom Ice Cream in a blender, you can make an Orange Blossom Freeze. Use approximately equal measurements of ice cream and ginger ale.

    4 cups whipping cream
    2½ cups granulated sugar
    ¼ teaspoon salt
    ¾ of a 6-ounce can of frozen orange-juice
        concentrate, undiluted
    ¼ cup lemon juice
    5 cups whole milk

Beat together the whipping cream, sugar, salt and orange juice concentrate. Add the lemon juice and milk. Freeze in an ice cream freezer. Makes about one gallon.

Fresh Peach Ice Cream

Peaches, probably native to China, have been consumed by man for over 3000 years. The ancient Romans sold peaches for what would be equivalent today to more than $4.50 apiece. On a hot summer day, when you are looking for a cool, refreshing dessert, Fresh Peach Ice Cream is what you need. Ripe peaches, blended with cream, a little sugar, and then frozen, will cool anyone's disposition.

    4 eggs
    2½ cups sugar
    5 cups whole milk
    3 cups whipping cream
    5 very ripe peaches
    1 tablespoon lemon juice

Blend the eggs and sugar thoroughly. Add the milk and cream and heat in a large pan over a medium-low flame, stirring frequently. When the mixture is hot to touch, about 110°F, remove from the stove and cool in refrigerator. Peel peaches and chop fine. Peaches must be very ripe (soft), or they will get caught in the dasher and cause problems. Add just enough sugar to take the tartness off

the peaches, then mix the chopped, sweetened peaches and the lemon juice. (The lemon juice brings out the flavor and keeps the peaches from turning dark.)

When the milk mixture has cooled, add the peaches. The best ice cream is obtained by cooling the whole mixture for a few hours before freezing.

Freeze in an ice cream freezer. Makes about one gallon.

Creamy Peach Ice Cream

Adding almond flavoring to a cream-rich peach ice cream creates a new and excitingly different taste sensation. This is also a good ice cream to keep in the freezing compartment of your refrigerator, since its flavor improves with time.

    2 cups sugar
    2 tablespoons cornstarch
    dash of salt
    2 eggs
    6 cups half-and-half
    2 teaspoons vanilla
    ½ teaspoon almond extract
    1 20-ounce package frozen sliced peaches
    sugar to sweeten peaches (about ½ cup)
    2 tablespoons lemon juice
    1 cup whole milk, or as needed

Thoroughly combine the sugar, cornstarch, salt and eggs. Stir in the half-and-half and cook over medium-low heat until the mixture thickens slightly. Remove from heat and refrigerate. When cool add the vanilla and almond extract.

Thaw the frozen peaches. Either dice them very small, or mash them with a potato masher. Add sugar to taste (about ½ cup). You should have 3 cups of sweetened mashed peaches. Mix in the lemon juice and refrigerate for at least 1 hour.

When you are ready to freeze the ice cream, add the peaches to the ice cream mixture and pour into the freezing can. Add enough whole milk to bring the level ¾ full. Churn and freeze. Makes about one gallon.

Pumpkin Ice Cream

Pumpkin Ice Cream is a seasonal treat, especially appropriate at times when people traditionally serve pumpkin pie: Thanksgiving and Christmas. As a matter of fact, when you are going to make pumpkin pie, make a double pumpkin custard recipe and turn the extra pie filling into ice cream. Just add extra sugar, cream and milk.

    1 16-ounce can pumpkin (2 cups)
    2 cups granulated sugar
    1 13-ounce can evaporated milk
    2 cups whipping cream

1 quart whole milk
2 eggs
½ teaspoon salt
1 teaspoon cinnamon
½ teaspoon ginger
¼ teaspoon cloves
4 teaspoons vanilla

In a large mixing bowl beat together all of the ingredients except the vanilla. Heat over medium-low heat until the mixture is very hot to touch (12 to 15 minutes cooking time). The heat blends the flavors and slightly thickens the mixture. Refrigerate until cool; add the vanilla and freeze in an ice cream freezer. Makes about one gallon.

Purple Plum Ice Cream

Little Jack Horner's Christmas pie would have been twice as good if he had had some tasty, homemade Purple Plum Ice Cream to go with it. Purple Plum Ice Cream is worth trying, whether you have a plum pie to eat alongside it or not.

2 1-pound, 14-ounce cans purple plums (about 32 plums)
¼ teaspoon almond extract
1 tablespoon lemon juice
2½ cups sugar
¼ teaspoon salt
7 cups half-and-half

Open two cans of purple plums and drain. Remove the seeds, add the almond extract and lemon juice to the plums and purée in a blender. Sweeten to taste (about ⅓ cup of sugar). Refrigerate the puréed plum mixture for a few hours to allow the flavors to blend.

In a large pan combine the sugar, eggs and salt, then add the half-and-half. Cook the mixture over medium-low heat, stirring constantly to prevent scorching. Remove the mixture from the stove when it is very hot to touch (about 150°F), and refrigerate until cool.

When you are ready to freeze the ice cream, combine the plum mixture with the milk mixture. Freeze in a home ice cream freezer. Makes about one gallon.

Raspberry Ice Cream

Raspberry Ice Cream makes a great dessert for any meal, its delicate taste and slight tartness adding a welcome finishing touch. It cleanses the palate with its light, flavorful smoothness and texture.

2⅔ cups sugar
4 eggs
5 cups whole milk
3 cups whipping cream
2½ cups mashed raspberries

1 tablespoon lemon juice
5 rennet tablets, dissolved in ¼ cup cold water

In a large pan blend together the sugar and eggs. Add 4 cups of whole milk and the whipping cream. While stirring, heat the mixture to approximately 110°F or until hot to touch. Remove mixture from the heat and let it cool in the refrigerator.

Mash the raspberries and blend in the lemon juice. Add the raspberries to the milk mixture. The longer the ice cream mixture is allowed to cool and blend the flavors, the smoother and better tasting your ice cream will be.

Ten minutes before freezing, add the dissolved rennet tablets and the remainder of the whole milk as needed to fill the freezing can ¾ full.

Churn and freeze. Makes about one gallon.

Two Berry Ice Cream

Two Berry Ice Cream will turn homemade ice cream skeptics into quick converts. The raspberry-blackberry combination used in this recipe came about quite by accident. While out picking wild raspberries one July, I came across some blackberries and threw them into the pail. The blend of red raspberries and blackberries is delicious.

6 cups whole milk
3 cups whipping cream
2½ cups granulated sugar
4 eggs, lightly beaten
2 cups wild red raspberries, mashed and sweetened
½ cup wild blackberries, mashed and sweetened
2 teaspoons vanilla extract
1 tablespoon lemon juice

In a large pan, combine the sugar, 1 quart of milk, whipping cream and beaten eggs. Heat the mixture over medium-low heat, stirring constantly, until it reaches approximately 130°F (or until the mixture feels very hot to your finger). Remove the mixture from the heat and cool in the refrigerator.

When the ice cream mixture has cooled, add the sweetened raspberries, sweetened blackberries, vanilla and lemon juice. Pour the mixture into the ice cream freezing can and add whole milk until the can is ¾ full.

Raspberries and blackberries are very seedy. If you like, you can remove most of the seeds by pushing the berries through a sieve or strainer.

Wild red raspberries and blackberries seem to have more flavor than their cultivated relatives, but domestic berries can be used. Fresh, frozen or canned berries will substitute for the fresh, wild ones.

If you use fresh raspberries and blackberries, use the quantities given in the recipe. Mash them, measure and sweeten to taste.

Two 10-ounce packages of frozen red raspberries can be used. Frozen berries are usually already sweetened. Thaw and mash the raspberries before using. Use all the juice, and decrease the amount of milk to compensate for the additional liquid. Either add half a 10-ounce package of frozen blackberries or half a 16-ounce can of blackberries.

Canned raspberries and blackberries can also be used. Add two 16-ounce cans of red raspberries and half a can of blackberries. Canned berries usually come in a sweetened syrup and do not require additional sugar. It may be advisable to drain off some of the liquid if the can seems to contain more liquid than berries. In any case, add enough whole milk to the mixture to fill the freezing can ¾ full. Makes about one gallon.

Strawberry Ice Cream

The strawberry is a native American plant and a relative of the rose, and it flavors the third most frequently consumed ice cream. Strawberry Ice Cream is good at any season. Frozen berries are easier to make ice cream with, since they are less firm than fresh berries and can be mashed more easily. Top your dish of Strawberry Ice Cream with sliced, fresh strawberries and you have a strawberry-strawberry sundae treat.

2⅔ cups granulated sugar
4 eggs
pinch of salt
3 cups whipping cream
3 cups mashed, sweetened strawberries (about ¼ cup sugar will sweeten berries)
1 tablespoon lemon juice
2 teaspoons vanilla extract
whole milk as needed (about 5 cups)

In a large pan combine the sugar, eggs and salt. Add the whipping cream and cook the mixture over medium-low heat, stirring constantly to avoid scorching. Remove from the heat when the mixture coats the back of a spoon (about 180°F). Refrigerate. When cool, add the vanilla.

Either dice the strawberries into very small pieces or slice and mash them. Add the lemon juice to the strawberries and stir in just enough sugar to sweeten (about ¼ cup). Refrigerate for at least 1 hour to allow the sugar to blend in with the strawberries.

When ready to freeze the ice cream, add the strawberries to the cream-sugar-and-egg mixture. Pour into an ice cream freezing can and add whole milk to bring the mixture up to ¾ full. Freeze in a home ice cream freezer. Makes about one gallon.

Nut Ice Cream Recipes

Almond Brickle Ice Cream

Almond Brickle Ice Cream tastes like toffee candy, with a crunchy goodness sure to be a big hit with your family.

    1½ cups sugar
    4 eggs, lightly beaten
    2 quarts half-and-half
    4 teaspoons vanilla
    2 7.8-ounce packages almond brickle chips

In a large pan, combine the sugar and eggs. Add the half-and-half and continue stirring while you slowly heat the mixture to about 160°F. Remove from the heat and refrigerate until completely cooled. Stir in the vanilla and almond brickle chips. Freeze in an ice cream freezer. Makes about one gallon.

Coffee Penuche Ice Cream

This is the first of three penuche ice cream recipes in this book. Penuche is a brown-sugar fudge, to which pecans are often added to improve the old-fashioned flavor.

    Coffee Penuche Ice Cream is best when eaten right after it has ripened. It becomes icy and very hard when stored in the freezing compartment of the refrigerator.

    4 tablespoons butter
    1 tablespoon instant coffee
    2⅔ cups packed brown sugar
    8 teaspoons water
    6 cups half-and-half
    2 cups whole milk
    4 eggs, lightly beaten
    ⅛ teaspoon salt
    1 tablespoon vanilla
    2 cups pecans, finely chopped

Melt the butter in a large pan over low heat. Add the instant coffee, brown sugar and water. Stir until the brown sugar and coffee are well blended into a thick paste.

    Increase the heat slightly and add the half-and-half, milk, eggs and salt. Stirring constantly, cook until the mixture is very hot (about 180°F). Remove from heat and cool in the refrigerator. Stir in the vanilla when cool.

    When ready to freeze, add the chopped pecans. Freeze in an ice cream freezer. Makes about one gallon.

Maple Penuche Ice Cream

Maple Penuche Ice Cream is made with a few ingredients not typically found in ice creams: maple syrup, brown sugar and butter are added for a special taste sensation.

    1½ cups brown sugar
    ¾ cup granulated white sugar
    3 eggs
    ¾ cup maple syrup
    6 cups half-and-half
    ¼ teaspoon salt

2 tablespoons butter or margarine
2 tablespoons vanilla
1⅔ cups pecans, finely chopped
whole milk as needed (about 2 cups)

In a large pan combine the brown sugar, white sugar and eggs. Stir in the maple syrup, half-and-half and salt. Cook over medium-low heat until the mixture thickens slightly (about 160°F). Stir constantly to prevent scorching.

Remove from heat and immediately stir in the butter. Cool in the refrigerator. When cool, stir in the vanilla.

When you are ready to freeze the ice cream mixture, add the chopped pecans. Pour the mixture into the freezing can, adding whole milk to fill ¾ full. Freeze in an ice cream freezer. Makes about one gallon.

Mexican Penuche Ice Cream

Pecans, dark brown sugar and a hint of chocolate are the special ingredients making Mexican Penuche Ice Cream just a step above other ice creams. If you are nutty about ice cream with nuts, you can't do without Mexican Penuche Ice Cream.

6 eggs
2½ cups firmly packed dark brown sugar
½ ounce unsweetened baking chocolate
1 quart whole milk
1 tablespoon butter or margarine
1 quart whipping cream
6 ounces (1½ cups) finely chopped pecans
4 teaspoons vanilla extract

In a large pan blend the eggs and dark brown sugar together to make a paste. Add the chocolate and whole milk; heat over medium-low heat until the chocolate melts and the mixture thickens slightly. Stir constantly to avoid scorching the mixture.

Remove from heat when the mixture has thickened somewhat, stir in the butter and refrigerate until cool.

Just before freezing in an ice cream freezer, add the whipping cream, chopped pecans and vanilla. Freeze in an ice cream freezer. Makes about one gallon.

Peanut Brittle Ice Cream

Combining a great candy with homemade ice cream leads to a unique taste temptation. Peanut Brittle Ice Cream is a crunchy delight for all the candy lovers in your family.

You can either make your own peanut brittle or purchase it. Either way, the most difficult part of this recipe is to keep from eating all the peanut brittle before it gets into the ice cream.

2½ cups sugar
4 eggs

2 quarts half-and-half
1 pound (3 cups) very finely crushed peanut brittle
4 teaspoons vanilla

Combine the sugar and eggs in a large pan. Add the half-and-half and cook over medium-low heat. Stir constantly to avoid scorching. Remove from heat when the mixture reaches about 140°F, and refrigerate until cool.

Break the peanut brittle into very small pieces. You can do this by placing the peanut brittle inside a heavy plastic bag and pushing a rolling pin over it.

When ready to freeze the ice cream mixture, add the peanut brittle and vanilla. Churn and freeze. Makes about one gallon.

Peanut Crunch Ice Cream

This is one of those smooth, delicious ice creams that looks simply terrible in the mixing pan. On the stove it is a curdly mess of ingredients that seemingly do not belong together. And once the hot ice cream mixture has cooled, kids' breakfast cereal is dumped in. How can it be? How can this bizarre concoction result in such a delicate blending of textures and tastes?

4 eggs
2½ cups sugar
2 cups crunchy peanut butter
1 quart half-and-half
1 tablespoon vanilla extract
4 cups Cocoa Rice breakfast cereal
whole milk as needed (3 to 4 cups)

Mix the eggs and sugar together in a large pan. Add the crunchy peanut butter and half-and-half. Stir continuously over medium-low heat until the peanut butter is blended and the mixture thickens (approximately 160°F).

Remove from heat and let the mixture cool in the refrigerator. When ready to freeze, add the vanilla, Cocoa Rice cereal and enough whole milk to bring the ice cream mixture to ¾ full in the freezing can. Makes about one gallon.

Happy turning and eating.

Rocky Road Ice Cream

Eating Rocky Road Ice Cream is like going on a treasure hunt, not for gold, silver and jewels, but for bits of chocolate, marshmallow and nuts.

2½ cups granulated sugar
4 eggs
5 cups whole milk
⅔ cup crunchy peanut butter
1 cup miniature marshmallows
2 cups whipping cream

4 teaspoons vanilla
1 cup miniature semisweet chocolate chips

In a large pan combine the sugar and eggs to make a thick paste. Add the milk and crunchy peanut butter. Stir constantly over low heat for 12 to 15 minutes, or until the mixture is very hot, but not boiling.

Remove pan from heat. Cool the mixture in the refrigerator.

Cut the miniature marshmallows into quarters. When the mixture has completely cooled and you are ready to churn the ice cream, stir in the cream, vanilla, marshmallows and chocolate chips.

Freeze in an ice cream freezer. Makes about one gallon.

Maple Walnut Ice Cream

The flavors produced by two trees give us Maple Walnut Ice Cream. The sweet sap of the sugar maple "runs" in the early spring, and is boiled to evaporate most of the water. What remains is delicious maple syrup. The stately walnut tree produces a yellow-green fruit containing a sweet nut. When the husk is dried and broken open, the nut meat can be removed.

2⅔ cups sugar
4 eggs
about 7 cups whole milk
3 cups whipping cream
2 cups finely chopped walnuts
2 teaspoons maple extract

Blend together the sugar and eggs to make a thick paste. Add about half the whole milk and all the whipping cream to the sugar-egg mixture. Heat the mixture over a medium-low flame, stirring to prevent scorching. Remove from heat when the mixture thickens (about 160°F). Refrigerate to cool. When ready to freeze, add the walnuts and maple extract. Pour the mixture into a freezing can and add whole milk to bring up to ¾ full.

Freeze in an ice cream freezer. Makes about one gallon.

Walnut Praline Ice Cream

Making Walnut Praline Ice Cream is a two-step process, beginning with the walnut pralines and followed by the ice cream base.

2 cups firmly packed brown sugar
3 cups walnuts, chopped
4 eggs, lightly beaten
2½ cups granulated sugar
5 cups half-and-half
¼ teaspoon salt
2 tablespoons vanilla

Put the brown sugar in a heavy skillet over low heat. Stir constantly and rapidly until it becomes a thick paste (about 30 minutes). The brown sugar will burn easily, so stir very rapidly near the end.

When the brown sugar has become a thick paste, turn off the heat and immediately stir in the chopped walnuts. Pour the hot sugar-and-walnut mixture onto waxed paper, spreading as thin as possible. Let cool and then crush into very small pieces.

To make the ice cream base, combine the eggs and granulated sugar in a large pan. Add the half-and-half and salt. Cook over medium-low heat until the mixture is very hot, but not boiling. Refrigerate until cool, then add vanilla.

When the ice cream is ready to freeze, add the walnut praline pieces and freeze in an ice cream freezer. Makes about one gallon.

Miscellaneous Ice Cream Recipes

Amaretto Ice Cream

Legend has it that the liqueur used to flavor this ice cream was first made in about 1525 by a beautiful Italian widow, who presented Amaretto as a gift to an artist from the school of Leonardo da Vinci. The artist, Bernardino Luini, was so impressed by the gift that he immortalized her in a now-famous fresco in the sanctuary of Santa Maria delle Grazie in Saronno.

This romantic Italian liqueur makes a delicious ice cream. Amaretto Ice Cream, while taking a little more preparation than other ice creams in this book, is well worth the effort. Made with plenty of egg yolks and whipped cream, a two-step freezing process creates this rich and fluffy taste treat.

> 8 egg yolks
> 1⅓ cups sugar
> 1 quart whole milk
> 1 cup whipping cream
> ¼ teaspoon vanilla extract
> ⅔ cup Amaretto liqueur

Combine egg yolks and sugar in a large mixing bowl. Beat with an electric mixer until stiff. Scald the milk. (Heat over medium-low heat to just below boiling, stirring constantly to avoid scorching.) While beating the egg-and-sugar mixture, slowly add the hot milk. Over low heat, stir the mixture until it coats the back of a spoon. Do not overheat. Keep the temperature under 200°F. Chill the mixture in the refrigerator, stirring occasionally.

Add the vanilla extract to the whipping cream and whip until stiff peaks form. Refrigerate.

Freeze the egg-sugar-milk mixture in an ice cream freezer, and remove the ice cream from the freezer when it has become thick and creamy. Scoop the frozen ice cream into a large bowl. Fold in the whipped cream and Amaretto. (The alcohol in the Amaretto will quickly melt the ice cream.) Pour mixture into a shallow freezing carton, cover and store in the freezing compartment of your refrigerator for at least 8 hours, or until frozen. It is then ready to serve and eat. Makes about one half gallon.

Butterscotch Ice Cream

Take a little butter and brown sugar, add heat and you have butterscotch syrup. It isn't quite that simple to make the very best Butterscotch Ice Cream you have ever tasted, but it isn't that difficult either.

> 1 stick (8 tablespoons) plus 2 tablespoons butter or margarine
> 3 cups packed brown sugar

2 quarts half-and-half
4 eggs, lightly beaten
¼ teaspoon salt
2 tablespoons vanilla

Melt the butter in a large pan over low heat. When melted, add the brown sugar. Continue to stir until the brown sugar just begins to caramelize (about 15 minutes).

Add the half-and-half, eggs and salt. Turn the heat up to medium-low, and stir constantly. Remove from heat when the mixture is very hot to touch and refrigerate until cold, then add vanilla. Freeze in an ice cream freezer. Makes about one gallon.

Butterscotch Chip Ice Cream

Butterscotch Chip Ice Cream is a tasty treat for any festive occasion. A buttery smooth ice cream is blended with just the right amount of candy-sweet chips. Serve Butterscotch Chip Ice Cream plain or sprinkle chopped pecans on top. For kids, serve graham crackers on the side or pour butterscotch sauce over the ice cream.

½ cup butter or margarine
3 cups packed dark brown sugar
4 cups milk, scalded
¼ teaspoon salt
3 eggs, lightly beaten
3 cups whipping cream
¼ cup flour
2 tablespoons vanilla extract
2 cups miniature butterscotch chips

Melt the butter in a large heavy pan. Add the brown sugar and stir over low heat until the sugar is melted and smooth. Slowly stir in the scalded milk, salt and eggs. Stir until the mixture is thoroughly blended. Combine the whipping cream and flour; mix well and add to the hot mixture. Continue to cook and stir until the mixture thickens slightly. Remove from the heat and chill. Add the vanilla and butterscotch chips to the cooled mixture just before freezing. Makes about one gallon.

Butterscotch Royal Ice Cream

Butterscotch gets its flavor from melted brown sugar and butter. To make Butterscotch Royal Ice Cream, follow the recipe below for butterscotch ice cream or use your favorite recipe. After the ice cream is frozen and firm, repack it in another container, layering in the butterscotch sauce.

½ cup butter
2½ cups packed brown sugar
7 cups half-and-half
4 eggs, lightly beaten
¼ teaspoon salt
5 teaspoons vanilla extract
2½ cups butterscotch sauce (see page 30)

Put the butter and brown sugar into a large, heavy pan. Stirring constantly with a wooden spoon, heat over medium-low heat until the brown sugar just begins to caramelize. Slowly stir in the half-and-half, eggs and salt. When the mixture reaches about 160°F, remove it from the stove. Refrigerate until cool, then add the vanilla. Freeze in an ice cream freezer.

When frozen, remove the dasher and repack with ice and salt for 2 or 3 hours. When the ice cream is firm, remove it from the freezing can and put it in a sealable container, alternating thin layers of ice cream with butterscotch sauce. Eat immediately or freeze in the freezing compartment of your refrigerator. Makes about one gallon.

Caramel Ice Cream

You do not often taste an ice cream as luscious as Caramel. Serve this to your friends and you will get raves and compliments. Caramel Ice Cream will soon be on your best-tasting list.

Caramel Ice Cream is not difficult to make, but it does take time to produce its special gourmet flavor. Allow an hour to make the mixture, since constant stirring is necessary to prevent scorching. Follow this recipe closely and you will have perfect Caramel Ice Cream.

Caramel syrup mixture
1 cup sugar
⅔ cup half-and-half

Ice cream mixture
3 eggs
1 cup sugar
4 cups half-and-half
pinch of salt
2 teaspoons vanilla extract

Put 1 cup of sugar in a heavy skillet and heat over medium-low burner. Stir constantly with a wooden spoon until the sugar turns into a deep, golden-brown, smooth syrup. This process takes 30 to 45 minutes. The sugar will be very lumpy before it melts and becomes a smooth syrup.

When the sugar has turned to a smooth, light brown syrup, slowly stir in ⅔ cup of very hot half-and-half. (It must be very hot or it will cause the melted sugar to become very hard. Do not worry if this happens. Just remelt the sugar over medium-low heat.) Stir over heat until the sugar and half-and-half are well blended, then remove from heat.

In a large pan combine the eggs and 1 cup of sugar. Stir until a thick paste is formed, then add 4 cups of half-and-half and a pinch of salt. Cook and stir over medium-low heat until the mixture is very hot (around 160°F). Slowly add the caramel syrup, mixing it in well. Remove the ice cream mixture from the heat and cool. Add the vanilla extract before freezing. Makes about one half gallon.

Coffee Ice Cream

According to legend, coffee was first discovered in the Ethiopian village of Kaffa. After eating red berries growing on a bush near the village, the inhabitants would start dancing. Word spread of the magical powers of the drink made by roasting and boiling the red berries. It wasn't until hundreds of years later that caffeine was discovered. The coffee bush grows easily and has been transplanted to many countries.

Coffee Ice Cream expands the coffee drinker's horizon. Now you can not only drink coffee, you can enjoy its flavor in ice cream as well. Enjoy your coffee hot, cold, in liquid or frozen form, any way you like it.

> 2⅔ cups sugar
> 4 eggs
> 2 tablespoons instant coffee
> ¼ teaspoon salt
> 6 cups whole milk
> 1 quart whipping cream
> 1 tablespoon vanilla extract

In a large pan combine the sugar, eggs, instant coffee and salt. Add the whole milk and cook over medium-low heat, stirring continuously to prevent scorching. Cook until the mixture thickens slightly (about 150°F).

Remove the mixture from the heat and refrigerate until cool, then add the whipping cream and vanilla.

Freeze in an ice cream freezer. Makes about one gallon.

Colorado Ice Cream

Add just a splash of a cola soft drink and crème de cacao liqueur to a vanilla ice cream mixture and voilà—Colorado Ice Cream, a frosty cold dessert with a kick.

> 4 eggs
> 2⅔ cups sugar
> 5 cups whole milk
> 3 cups whipping cream
> 2 tablespoons vanilla extract
> ½ cup crème de cacao liqueur
> 1½ cups cola soft drink

Combine the eggs and sugar to make a thick paste. Add the whole milk and, while stirring constantly, cook over medium-low heat.

When the mixture is hot, about 150°F, remove from the stove and refrigerate until cool.

Just before freezing in an ice cream freezer, add the whipping cream and vanilla. Pour the mixture into the freezing can and begin freezing.

When the mixture is partly frozen, remove the lid of the freezing can and pour in the crème de cacao and the cola. Replace the lid and continue to churn until frozen. Makes about one gallon.

NOTE: If you would like to try Colorado Ice Cream but do not want to make a freezer full, here's a suggestion. In a blender whip together about ⅔ cup of vanilla ice cream, 2 teaspoons of crème de cacao and a splash of cola (2 tablespoons). Drink it just as it comes from the blender, or freeze it in an airtight container in your freezer. Makes about one cup.

Eggnog Ice Cream

Eggnog, a popular holiday-season drink, can also be a delicious, easy-to-make ice cream. Add interest to your holiday eggnog by serving it frozen. In season, eggnog can be purchased from the dairy case of your neighborhood grocer. If you wish, use your favorite eggnog recipe instead.

> 2 quarts eggnog
> 2⅔ cups half-and-half
> 1⅓ cups granulated sugar
> 2 teaspoons vanilla extract

Pour all ingredients into the freezing can and freeze. Makes about one gallon.

Honey Bee Ice Cream

Honey, made by bees from the nectar of flowers, has been used by man as a sweetener and a food since prehistoric times. (Sugar was not widely used as a sweetener until the seventeenth century.) Honey still plays an important role as a sweetener and food for man. Follow this recipe for an excellent-tasting ice cream. The gelatin is needed because honey contains a substance that inhibits freezing.

> 2 packages (2 tablespoons) unflavored gelatin
> ½ cup packed brown sugar
> ⅛ teaspoon salt
> 1 teaspoon cinnamon
> 8 cups half-and-half
> 4 eggs, lightly beaten
> 2½ cups honey
> 2 teaspoons vanilla extract

In a large pan, mix the gelatin, brown sugar, salt and cinnamon. Add 4 cups of the half-and-half and the eggs, and heat over a medium-low flame, stirring constantly, until the gelatin is completely dissolved and the mixture is very hot, but not boiling.

Remove the mixture from the heat and stir in the

honey. Then add the remainder of the half-and-half and the vanilla.

Freeze in an ice cream freezer. Makes about one gallon.

Jello Ice Cream

When you are writing a cookbook all of your friends and relatives give you their favorite recipes to try. For fear of an inadvertent copyright infringement, I have thanked them for their recipes, but have not included them in this book. There is one exception, however. My brother gave me the following recipe for Jello Ice Cream. He claims it came about from a free-for-all kitchen spree when he and his mother-in-law decided to make ice cream. Finding the kitchen bare of the usual ice cream ingredients, they concocted their own recipe, ad-libbing as they went. After hearing about the development of this recipe and after looking at it, I am sure it is original. Only my brother could have come up with something as strange as Jello Ice Cream.

    2 eggs, separated
    1 large (6-ounce) package fruit-flavored gelatin, any
        flavor
    2 rennet tablets
    1 cup mashed fruit (fruit and gelatin may be the same
        flavor, or complement each other)
    ½ cup sweetened condensed milk
    ⅔ cup sugar
    about 10 cups half-and-half

Separate the egg whites from the yolks. Beat the egg whites until stiff. Dissolve the flavored gelatin in ¼ cup of boiling water. Stir until dissolved. Dissolve the rennet tablets in 2 tablespoons cold water.

In a large bowl, fold the egg whites into the sweetened condensed milk. Gradually add the sugar. Fold in the mashed fruit, egg yolks, flavored gelatin and rennet tablets. Pour the mixture into the freezing can. Add the half-and-half to fill the freezing can to the proper level.

Freeze in an ice cream freezer. Makes about one gallon.

Instant Butter Pecan Ice Cream

A quick and easy way to make ice cream is by using instant pudding mixes. No cooking is required. This method is especially convenient for picnics and camping trips where heating an ice cream mixture may be difficult. This recipe uses instant butter pecan pudding, but any instant pudding will work. Instant Butter Pecan Ice Cream will not expand during the freezing process as most other ice creams do. You can, therefore, fill the freezer can a little fuller than normal. Also, this ice cream will freeze fast and firm.

For another ice cream using instant pudding, try the next recipe, Pistachio Nut Pudding Ice Cream, which has a different taste, richer and not as sweet.

    2 3⅝-ounce packages instant butter pecan pudding
        mix
    1 cup granulated sugar
    2 13-ounce cans evaporated milk
    6 cups whole milk
    2 teaspoons vanilla

Mix all the ingredients together and immediately pour into freezing can and freeze. Makes about one gallon.

Pistachio Nut Pudding Ice Cream

This is a recipe using an instant pudding mix for flavor and body. The result is a quick, sweet-tasting ice cream with a pudding taste. No cooking is necessary. Unlike Instant Butter Pecan Ice Cream just above, this ice cream mixture will expand during the freezing process.

    2 3⅝-ounce packages instant pistachio nut pudding
        mix
    1 can sweetened condensed milk
    1 13-ounce can evaporated milk
    about ½ gallon whole milk

In a large mixing bowl, beat together the pudding mix, sweetened condensed milk and evaporated milk. Pour into freezing can and add whole milk to bring mixture to ¾-full mark. Freeze immediately. Makes about one gallon.

Peanut Butter Chip Ice Cream

This recipe incorporates the taste of a peanut butter candy bar in a creamy smooth ice cream. You'll enjoy the unusual taste brown sugar adds.

    2½ cups packed brown sugar
    4 eggs
    ⅛ teaspoon salt
    2 quarts half-and-half
    2 tablespoons vanilla extract
    2 cups (1 12-ounce package) peanut butter chips

In a large pan blend together the brown sugar, eggs and salt. Add the half-and-half and heat over a medium-low flame. Stir constantly to avoid scorching. Remove the mixture from the heat when the brown sugar has dissolved and the mixture is very hot (about 150°F).

Refrigerate the mixture until it cools; then add the vanilla and peanut butter chips.

Freeze in an ice-cream freezer. Makes about one gallon.

Creamy Peanut Butter and Chips Ice Cream

Take delicious peanut butter chips; add yummy peanut butter and ice cream. What could be a better after-school treat for kids or a work break for adults? Don't tell anyone, but besides tasting wonderful, Creamy Peanut Butter and Chips Ice Cream is high in nutritional value. It is great on the taste buds and an energy pick-me-up besides.

2½ cups sugar
4 eggs
1 cup smooth peanut butter
7 cups half-and-half
5 teaspoons vanilla
2 cups (1 12-ounce package) peanut butter chips

Assemble the ingredients. Get out a large pan. Blend together the sugar, eggs and peanut butter. Add the half-and-half and heat over medium-low heat. Be sure to stir the mixture to avoid scorching. Remove it from the heat when the mixture is very hot to touch (about 140°F).

Refrigerate until the ice cream mixture has cooled.

Add the vanilla and peanut butter chips when you are ready to freeze the ice cream mixture. Makes about one gallon.

White Licorice Ice Cream

A good friend of mine is fond of licorice candy. She kept asking me, half-teasingly and half-seriously, to make licorice ice cream for her. After repeated requests, I developed the following recipe. Now all she says is, "Why isn't it black?"

4 eggs
2⅔ cups sugar
about 7 cups whole milk
3 cups whipping cream
1 teaspoon anise flavoring

Blend the eggs and sugar together well in a large pan.

Add about half of the milk and all of the cream. Cook over medium-low heat to blend flavors, stirring to prevent scorching. Heat for about 12 to 15 minutes or until mixture is very hot to touch. Remove from heat and refrigerate.

After the mixture has cooled, add the anise flavoring. Pour the mixture into the freezing can and add whole milk as needed to fill the can ¾ full.

Freeze in an ice cream freezer. Makes about one gallon.

Ice Cream Toppings

Marshmallow Sauce

1 cup sugar
½ cup water
15 marshmallows
3 egg whites
¾ teaspoon vanilla

Boil the sugar and water for 10 minutes to make a thin syrup. Reduce heat and add the marshmallows. Stir until marshmallows are melted and mixture is smooth. Remove from heat. Beat the egg whites until stiff peaks are formed; then slowly beat in the marshmallow syrup. Continue whipping until smooth and fluffy. Fold in the vanilla. Store in the refrigerator in a container with a tight-fitting lid. Serve hot or cold. Makes 1⅔ cups.

Butterscotch Sauce

1¼ cups packed brown sugar
¼ cup butter
½ cup corn syrup
½ cup evaporated milk
¾ teaspoon vanilla

Put the brown sugar, butter and corn syrup in a heavy saucepan and heat to boiling, stirring constantly. Remove the mixture from the heat, stir in the evaporated milk and vanilla, and beat until smooth. Refrigerate in a closed container. Serve warm. Makes 1¼ cups.

Caramel Sauce

1 cup sugar
⅔ cup half-and-half

Put the sugar in a heavy saucepan and place over medium-low heat. Stir constantly with a wooden spoon until the sugar turns to a smooth, golden-brown syrup. This process will take 30 to 45 minutes. The sugar will be very lumpy before it melts and becomes a smooth syrup.

When the sugar has turned to syrup, slowly stir in ⅔ cup of very hot half-and-half. The half-and-half must be very hot or it will cause the melted sugar to become hard and lumpy. (Do not worry if this happens. Just remelt the sugar over medium-low heat). Stir over heat until the sugar and half-and-half are well blended, then remove from the heat.

Store the caramel sauce in the refrigerator in a sealed container. Serve hot.

Chocolate Sauce

6 tablespoons cocoa
¾ cup sugar
2 tablespoons flour
⅛ teaspoon salt
1 cup milk
3 tablespoons butter
¾ teaspoon vanilla

Combine the dry ingredients; add the milk. Cook over medium-low heat until the mixture begins to thicken (about 8 minutes). Remove the pan from the heat and stir in the butter and vanilla. Store in a sealed container in the refrigerator. Serve hot or cold. Makes about 2 cups.

Chocolate Fudge Sauce

2 squares unsweetened chocolate
1 tablespoon butter
⅔ cup evaporated milk
1 cup sugar
⅛ teaspoon salt
2 teaspoons vanilla

Break the chocolate squares into small pieces and melt with the butter in a saucepan over low heat. Increase the heat to medium-low and gradually add the evaporated milk, sugar and salt. Stir and cook until the mixture just begins to boil. Remove the chocolate sauce from the heat and let cool slightly. Stir in the vanilla and store in the refrigerator. Heat before serving. Makes 1⅓ cups.

Peanut Butter Sauce

½ cup chunky peanut butter
½ cup maple syrup

Mix the peanut butter and maple syrup together and pour over ice cream. May be served hot or cold. Makes one cup.

Other Ice Cream Topping Ideas

Almond Brickle
Breakfast Cereals: Grapenuts, Cocoa Crispies, Rice Crispies, Shredded Wheat
Butterscotch Chips
Butterscotch Sauce
Candy, crushed
Caramel Sauce
Chocolate Brownies, crumbled
Chocolate Chips
Chocolate Fudge Sauce
Chocolate Syrup
Coconut
Coffee Syrup
Crème de Menthe
Dry Macaroons, crushed
Fruits: Bananas, Blackberries, Blueberries, Cherries, Peaches, Pineapple, Raspberries, Strawberries, etc.
Honey
Hot Fudge Sauce
Maple Syrup
Marshmallows
Marshmallow Creme
Mint Sticks, finely crushed
Nuts of all kinds
Ovaltine
Peanut Brittle
Peanut Butter Chips
Peanut Butter Sauce
Pineapple Topping
Powdered Chocolate Drink Mix
Pudding, various flavors